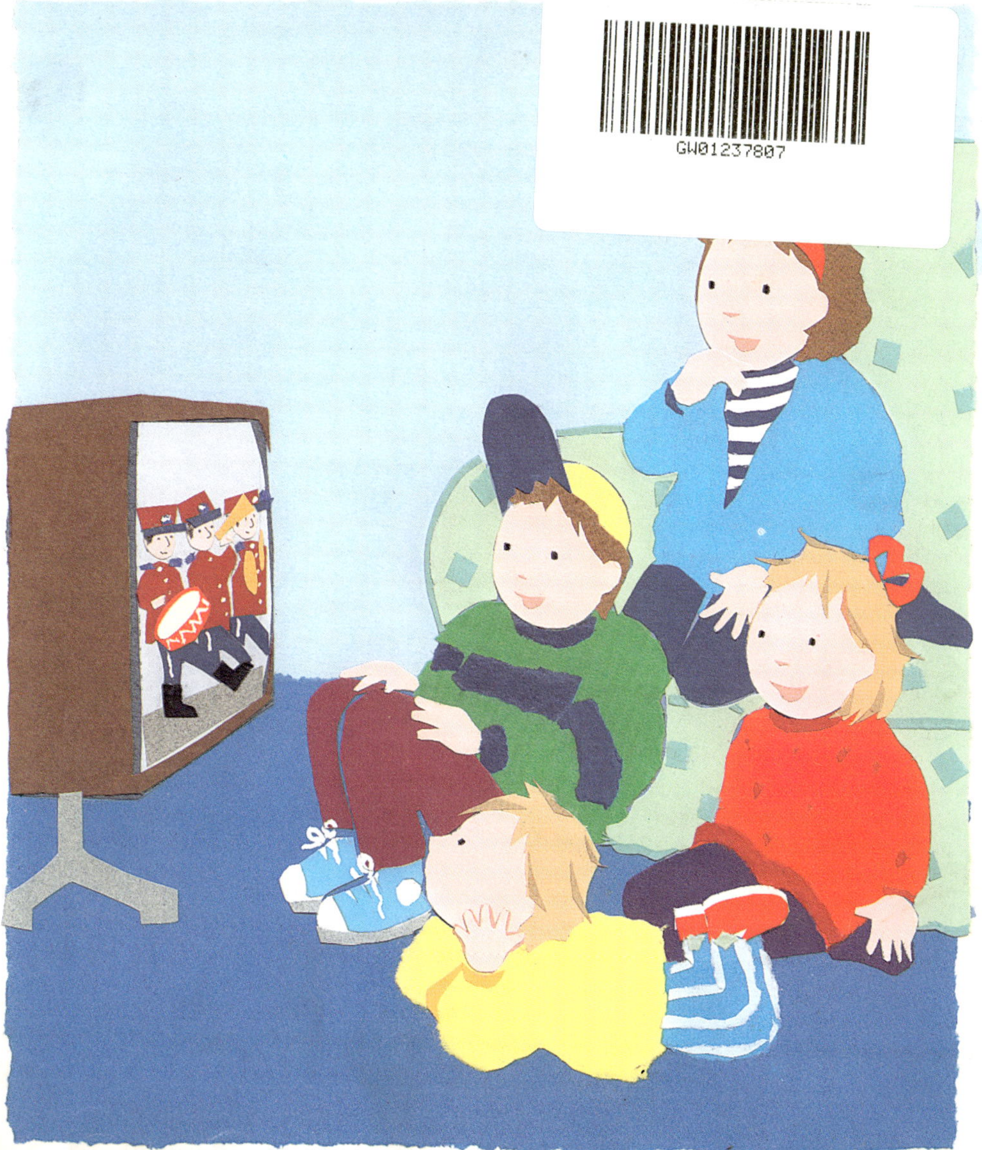

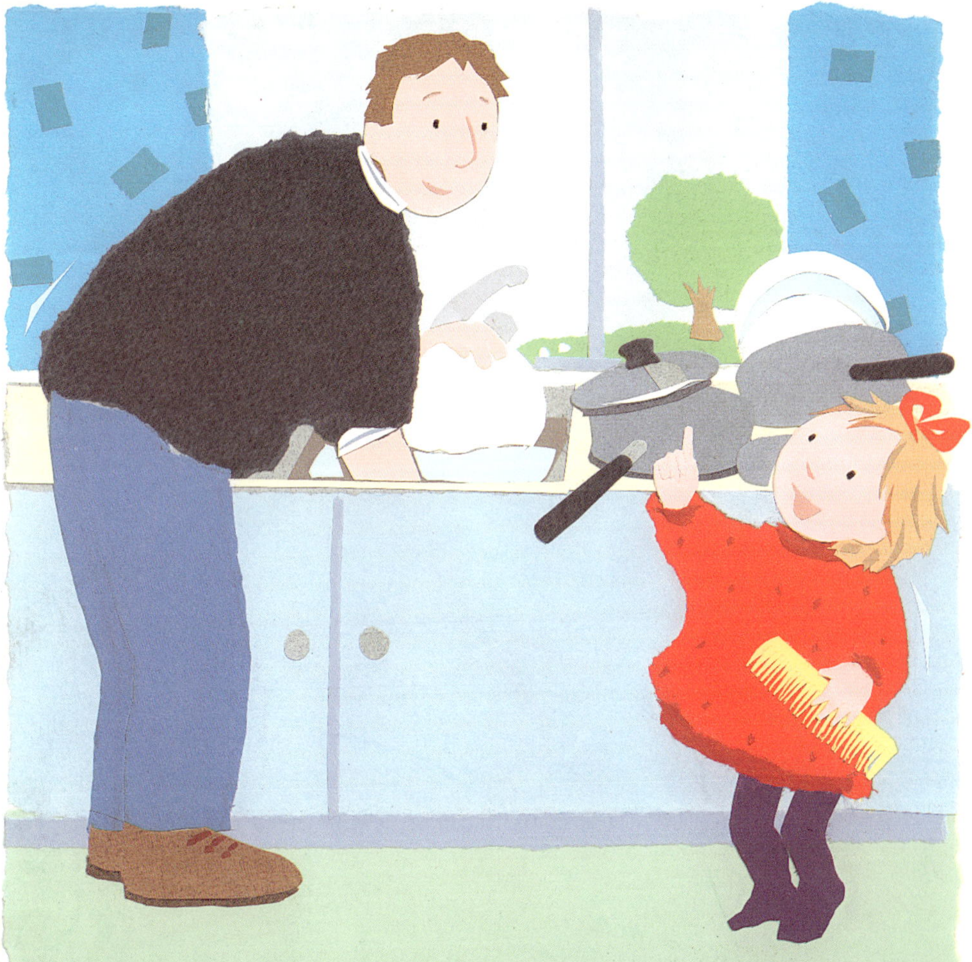

"Dad, can I have these pans?"

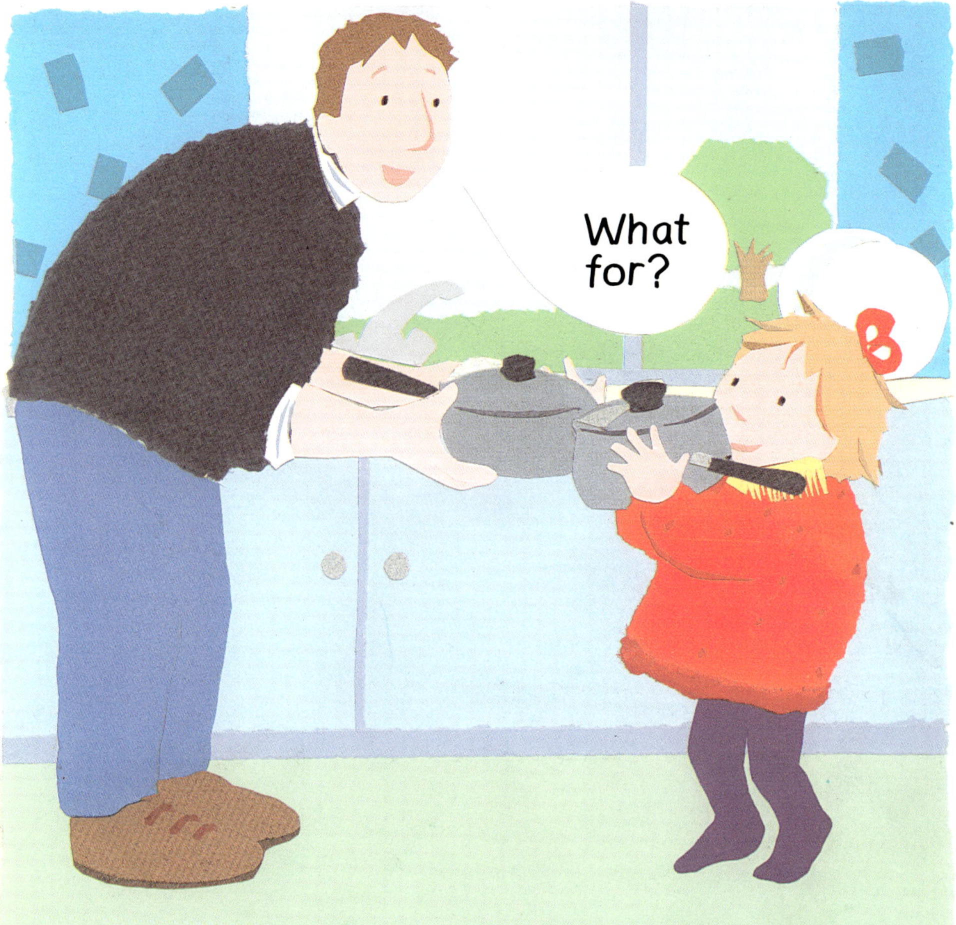

"What for?"

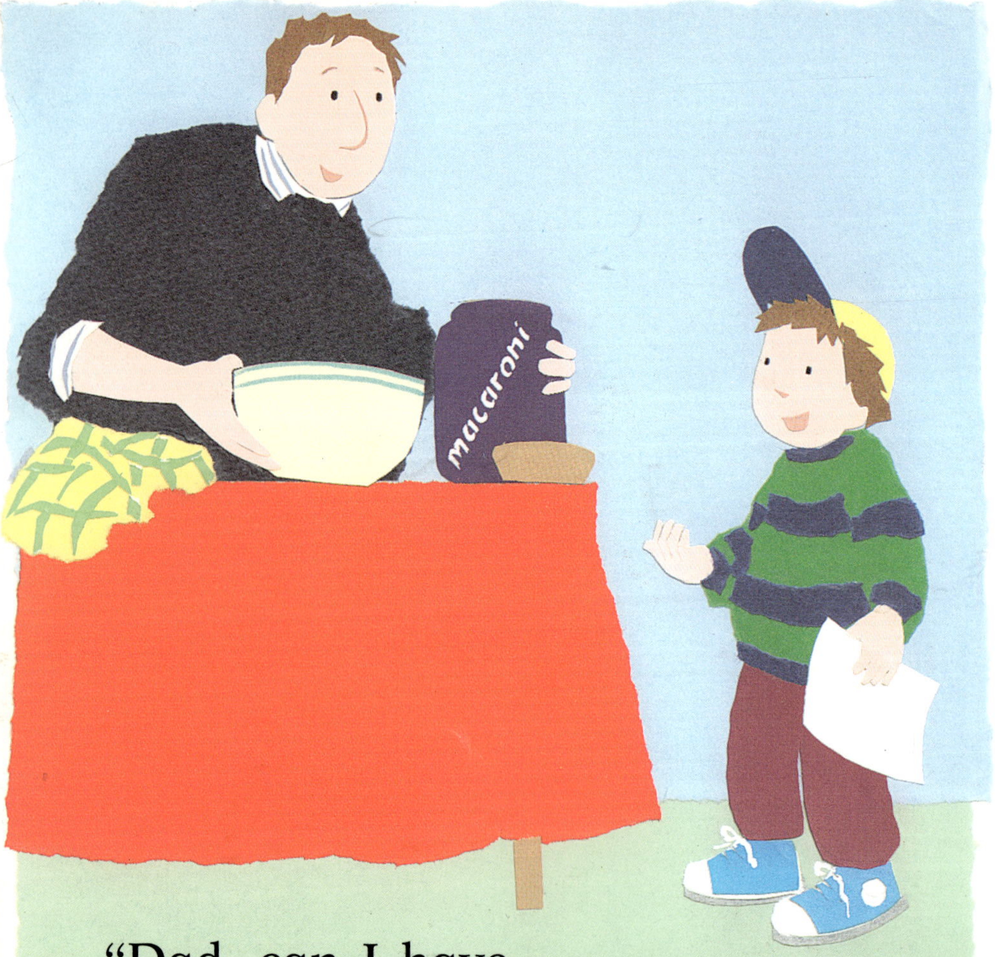

"Dad, can I have
some macaroni?"

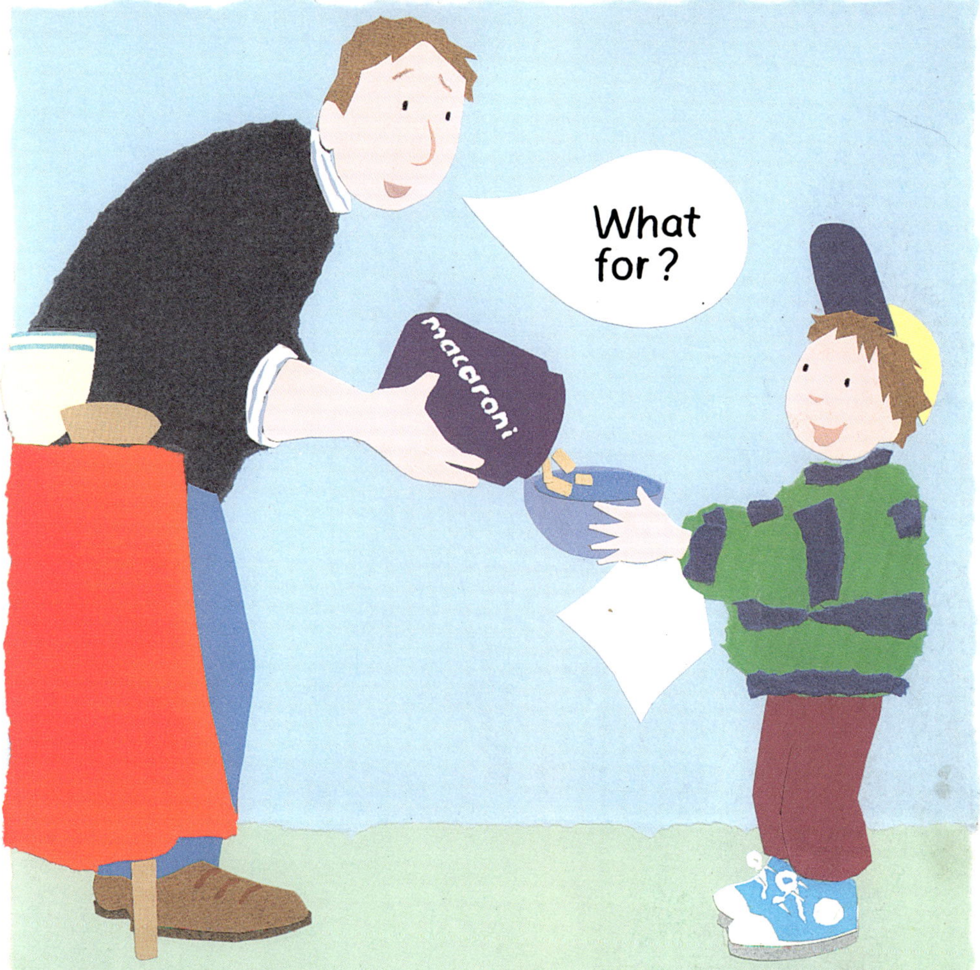

"What for?"

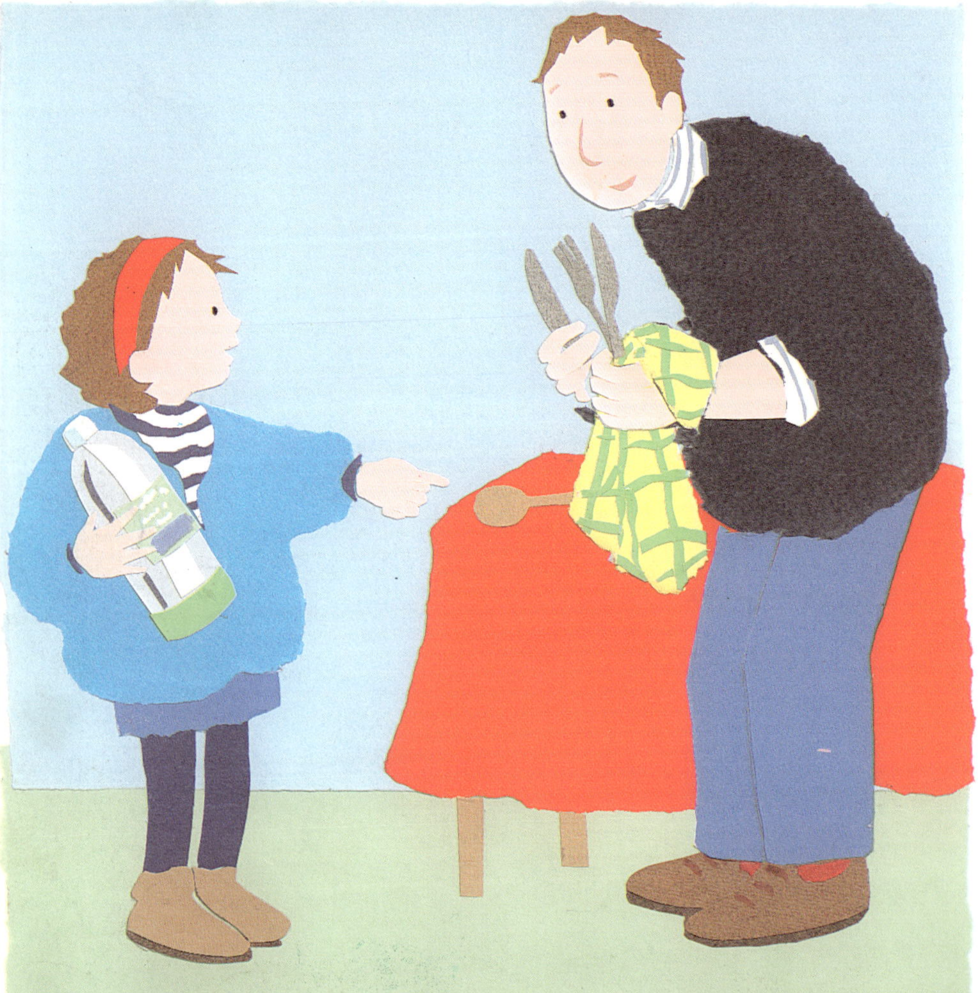

"Dad, can I have this spoon?"

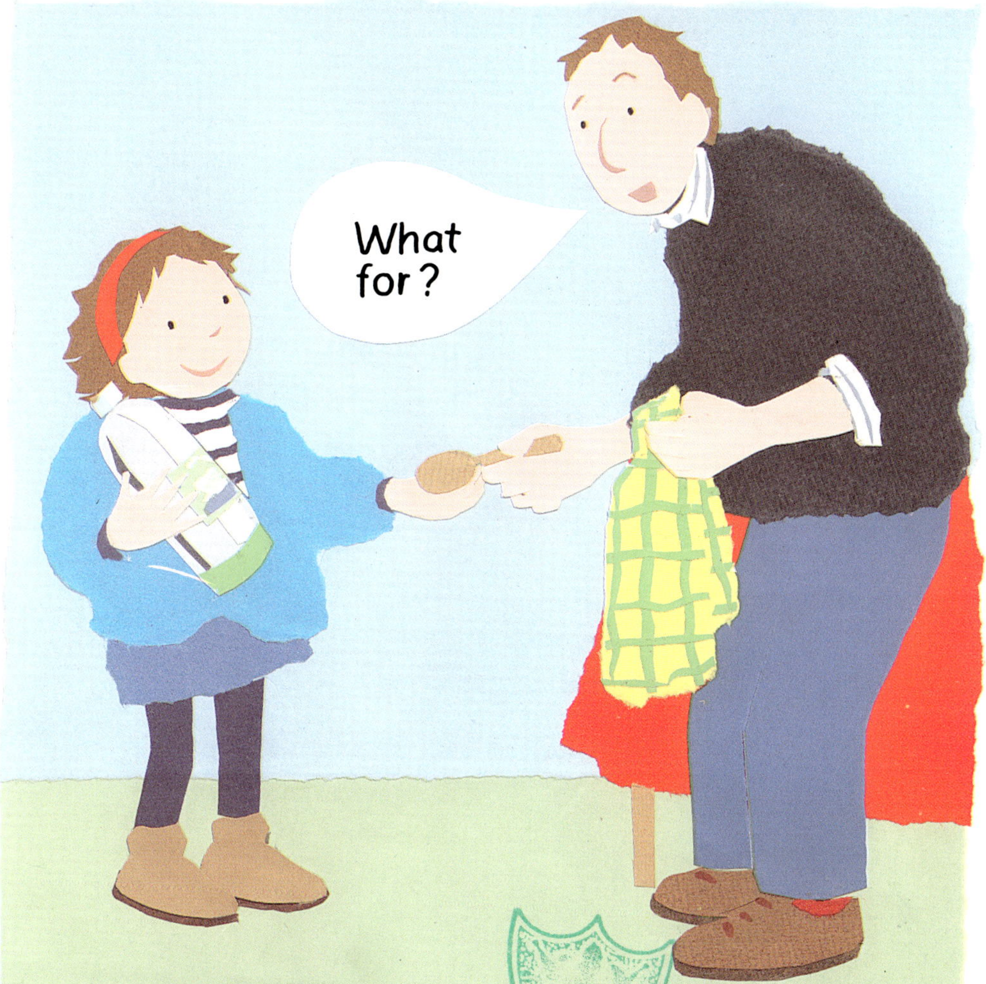

“What for?”

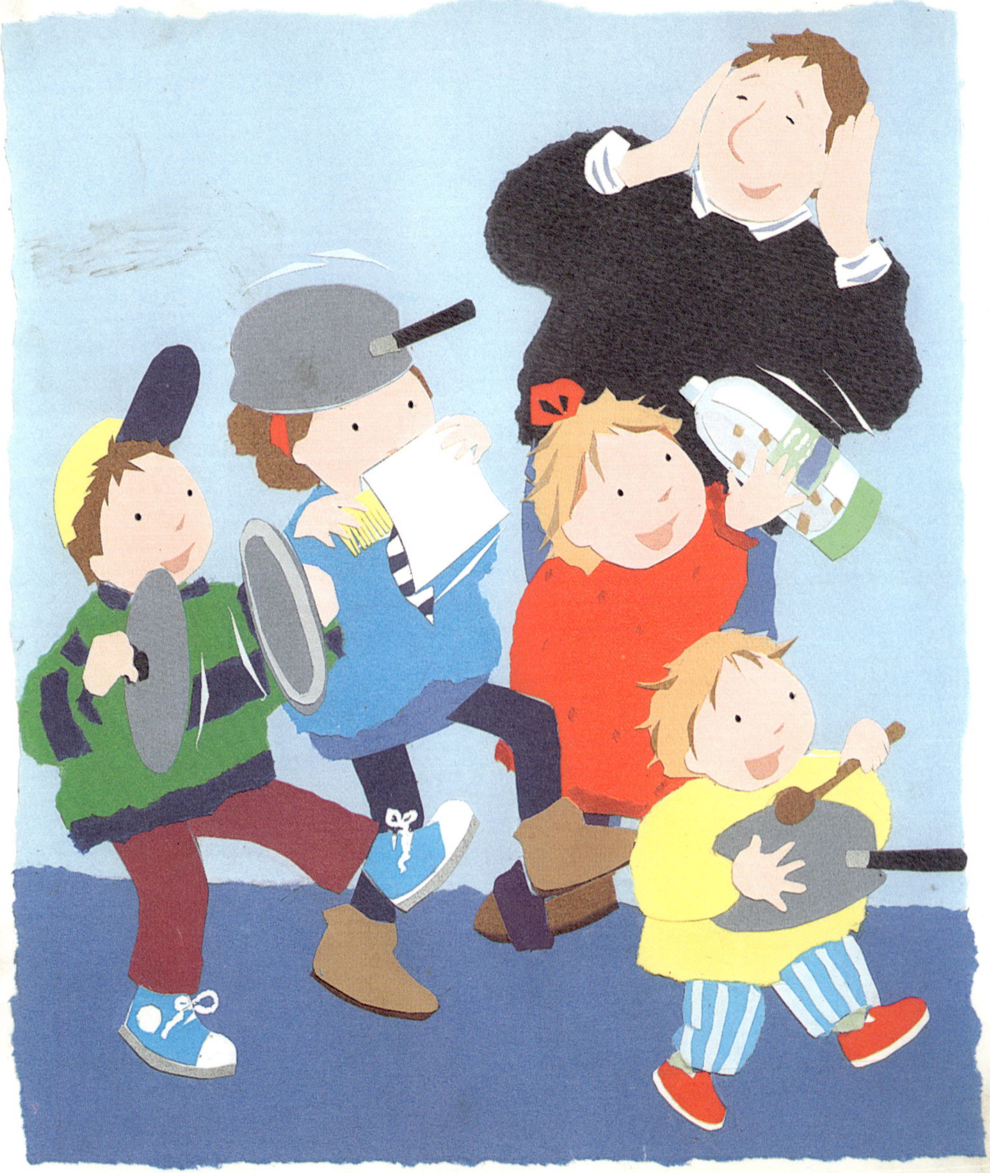